Contents

T0351693

Written by
David Grant

Illustrated by
Dylan Gibson
and **Andy Stephens**

Series editor **Dee Reid**

Pearson

Characters

Kris

Emma

Jake

Kelly

Tricky words

- breaktime
- smiled
- fancies
- beautiful
- pale
- croaked
- weird
- lied

Read these words to the student. Help them with these words when they appear in the text.

Introduction

Kris and Jake are best mates. Kelly is in their year at school. She is a computer genius. Most of the time, Kris and Jake get on well with Kelly but sometimes they are not sure about what she is up to on her computer. One day, Kris and Jake were in the canteen. Kelly walked past and smiled at Jake. Kris thought Kelly fancied Jake. Then Emma, who Kris and Jake really fancied, ran up and slapped Jake across the face.

The Hacker

It was breaktime.

Kris and Jake were in the canteen.

Kelly walked past them and smiled at Jake.

"Why does Kelly keep smiling at you?" asked Kris.

"I don't know," said Jake.

"Maybe she fancies you!" said Kris.

"Shut up!" said Jake.

"Yesterday, Kelly was asking me all about you," said Kris. "She wanted to know what your pets were called and if you had a girlfriend. She must be up to something."

Just then Emma came running up.
She looked angry.
Jake and Kris both thought Emma
was the most beautiful girl in the school.
They really fancied her.
To Jake's surprise, Emma slapped
him across the face.

"What was that for?" asked Jake, rubbing his cheek.
"Get the message," Emma shouted. She pointed
her finger in Jake's face. "I don't want to go
out with you. Is that clear?"
Jake went pale.
"Yes," he croaked.
"Good," said Emma. And she walked off.

"When did you ask Emma out?" asked Kris.

"I didn't!" said Jake.

"That is really weird," said Kris.

"But that's not the only weird thing," said Jake. "I've been getting messages from Emma."

"Like what?" asked Kris.

"Things like, 'Stop sending me messages' and 'Leave me alone'," said Jake.

"What kind of messages have you been sending her?" asked Kris.

"That's another weird thing," said Jake. "I haven't been sending Emma any messages."

"I think someone's got into your email account and sent messages to Emma, pretending that they came from you," said Kris.

"Who could do that?" asked Jake.

"Someone who knows your password," said Kris.

"I would never tell anyone my password," said Jake.

Then Kris had an idea.

"Hang on," he said. "I've just remembered. Kelly was asking me all those questions about you. About your pet's name and things like that."

Jake went red.

"Is your password your dog's name?" asked Kris.

"It might be," said Jake.

"Well that's it then," said Kris. "Kelly has worked out your password and got into your account."

That lunchtime, Jake was waiting for Kelly outside the hall.

"Oi!" shouted Jake when he saw her. "Come here!"

Kelly came over.

"Have you been hacking into my email account?" said Jake.
He looked really angry.

"What if I have?" said Kelly, smiling. "It'll teach you a lesson. You should come up with a better password."

"You'll get into big trouble for this," said
Jake. "I'll tell someone. I'll tell the police."
Kelly laughed.
"You could," she said, "Or I could help you play
some jokes. I can get into anyone's computer
and do anything I like on it."
"Really?" asked Jake.
"Really," said Kelly.

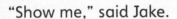

"Show me," said Jake.

"OK," said Kelly. "You tell Kris that I didn't hack into your email account. And I'll tell you what we're going to do."

"What are we going to do?" asked Jake.

"We're going to play a joke on Kris," said Kelly.

Kris came up just as Kelly was leaving.
"She says she didn't hack into my email account," Jake lied.
"I wonder who it was then," said Kris.
"I don't know," said Jake, trying not to smile.

The next day, Kris looked really happy
– until breaktime.
That was when Emma came up.
This time she slapped Kris across the face.
Then she walked off.

"What was that about?" asked Jake.
"I got an instant message from Emma last night," said Kris. "She said she wanted to go out with me. So I sent her one back. I said I wanted to go out with her too. But I think she's changed her mind now."

Jake smiled.
Kelly wasn't lying, he thought.
She can do anything when she gets on a computer.

Quiz /////////////////////////

Text comprehension

Literal comprehension
p5–7 Why did Emma slap Jake across the face?
p10 Why did Kelly hack into Jake's email account?

Inferential comprehension
p13 Why does Jake try not to smile when Kris wonders who hacked into Jake's account?
p15 What makes Kris think Emma has changed her mind about going out with him?
p15–16 What joke did Kelly play on Kris?

Personal response
- How would you feel if someone hacked into your email account?
- Do you think the joke Kelly played on Kris was funny or cruel? Why?

Word knowledge

p6 Why has the author used the word 'croaked'?
p8 Which word joins the two parts of the first sentence?
p14 What punctuation is used in the first sentence?

Spelling challenge

Read these words:

only   turned   huge

Now try to spell them!

Ha! Ha! Ha!

What do you call a computer super hero?

A Screen Saver

Find out about

- We use passwords to protect our accounts, but how safe are some passwords?

Tricky words

- private
- guards
- guess
- favourite

- dictionary
- lower case
- scientists
- sentence

Read these words to the student. Help them with these words when they appear in the text.

Introduction

Most people have passwords to stop other people seeing private things on their mobile or computer. But passwords don't stop hackers. Hackers can get into your email and social networking websites and find out your password so you should choose a password the hacker can't work out by guessing.

What's the Password?

Do you have a password?
Do you use it to stop other people
seeing private things on your
mobile or computer?

Passwords are not a new idea. Hundreds of years ago the guards at a palace would ask people to give a password before they could get in to see the king.

What's the password?

Hackers

You might think your details are safe because you use a password.

But passwords don't stop hackers!

Hackers can get into email and social networking websites and find out your password.

Sometimes they even put your password on the internet to show how clever they are.

Loads of people have just one password and they use that password for lots of different websites.

So if a hacker finds out your password they can get into all of your accounts.

And that's not all!

Loads of people choose the same passwords which makes it really easy for hackers to guess them.

roversrgreat

arsena

upmanu

TOP SECURITY

Popular passwords

Lots of people choose the name of someone in their family or the name of a pet as their password. Sometimes people choose the name of their favourite football team or a character from a film. The word 'monkey' is also a very popular password, but no one seems to know why!

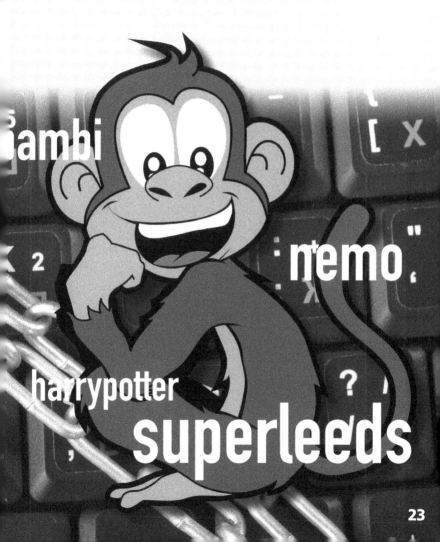

The most popular password which uses only letters is: **password**

The most popular password which uses letters and numbers is: **password1**

People think that passwords which use numbers and letters are safer but most people just put the number I at the end of their password.

This is not a good idea as it is the first thing hackers try when they want to get past your password.

Beat the computer!

If a hacker cannot work out your password by guessing they can use a computer program. First, the computer program tries every word in the dictionary. If that doesn't work, it starts trying random letters and numbers.

A normal computer running one of these programs can try up to 10 million different passwords every second.
If your password was 1 2 3 4 5 6, it would take just 10 seconds to work it out!
But if your password used capital letters, lower case letters and numbers, the same computer would take 253 days to guess it.

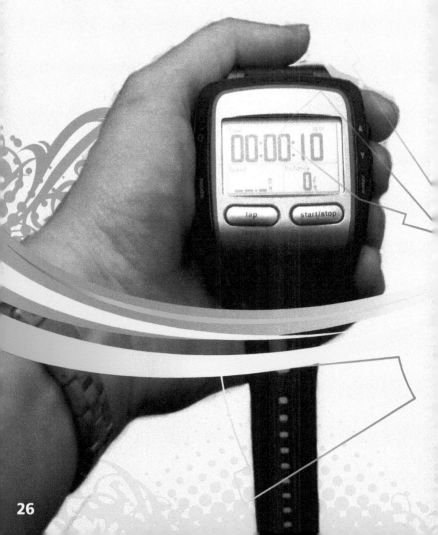

Listening hard

It's not just computer programs that can guess your password.

Some people can work out your password just by listening to you as you type it into a computer.

Scientists in America discovered that they could train people to hear the letters and numbers that were being typed.

They found that you can work out a short password in about 20 guesses just by hearing it being typed.

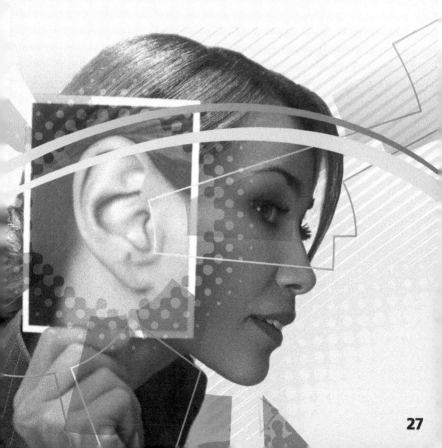

The best passwords

Experts say that your password should use at least 8 letters and numbers.
You should use a mixture of capital letters, lower case letters and numbers.
You should not use just one word by itself.
Two words are much harder to guess.

j4dH3A9m

Eg6p2Zj7

zB84gQ2p

kH45dAz9f

Xw8nM24k

h5V4aLq3

V5r7d2sN

Y8gD32vX

Even better is to use the first letters of 8 or 9 words in a sentence which you can easily remember. So, if you can remember the sentence 'Liverpool won the FA Cup in 2006', you could make your password 'LwtFACi2006' which is very difficult to guess.

You should also use different passwords for different accounts. Don't use the same password for Facebook as you use for Twitter!

In 2009, the website RockYou.com was broken in to. The passwords of 32 million people were posted on the internet. These were the most popular:

Top 10 passwords

1	123456
2	12345
3	123456789
4	password
5	iloveyou
6	princess
7	rockyou
8	1234567
9	12345678
10	Abc123

Nearly 300,000 people were using the most popular password.
Is your password in the top 10?
If it is, it probably won't be long before someone hacks you.
So watch out!
Think hard and choose carefully when making up a password.

Quiz ////////////////////

Text comprehension

Literal comprehension
p22 Why should you not have the same password for lots of websites?

p25–26 Why should you have capital letters, lower case letters and numbers in your password?

Inferential comprehension
p21 Why might hackers want to get into your email and social networking websites?

p23 Why do loads of people choose the same passwords?

p27 Why might it not be a good idea to let people hear you enter your password?

Personal response
• Do you have one of the top ten passwords?
• Will you change your password after reading this book?

Word knowledge

p23 Find two adjectives.
p27 Find a word that means 'found out'.
p31 Find an adverb.

Spelling challenge

Read these words:

family   running   those

Now try to spell them!

Ha! Ha! Ha!

Why did the computer squeak?

Because someone stepped on its mouse!